Successful Subject Co-ordination

Other Classmates:

2nd Series
Parent Partnership in the Early Years –
Damien Fitzgerald
Playing Outdoors in the Early Years – Ros Garrick
Assemblies Made Easy – Victoria Kidwell
Homework – Victoria Kidwell
Getting Promoted – Tom Miller
ICT in the Early Years – Mark O'Hara
Creating Positive Classrooms – Mike Ollerton
Getting Organized – Angela Thody and
Derek Bowden
Physical Development in the Early Years –
Lynda Woodfield

1st Series
Lesson Planning – Graham Butt
Managing Your Classroom – Gererd Dixie
Teacher's Guide to Protecting Children – Janet Kay
Tips for Trips – Andy Leeder
Stress Busting – Michael Papworth
Every Minute Counts – Michael Papworth
Teaching Poetry – Fred Sedgwick
Running Your Tutor Group – Ian Startup
Involving Parents – Julian Stern
Marking and Assessment – Howard Tanner

Successful Subject
Co-ordination

Christine Farmery

continuum
LONDON • NEW YORK

Continuum

The Tower Building
11 York Road
London SE1 7NX

15 East 26th Street
New York
NY 10010

British Library Cataloguing-in-Publication Data
A catalogue record for this book is available from the British Library.

ISBN 0–8264–7240–0 (paperback)

Typeset by BookEns Ltd, Royston, Herts.
Printed and bound in Great Britain by
Antony Rowe Ltd., Chippenham, Wiltshire

For my husband
Peter Farmery
for all his patience and support

Contents

1

Towards a Definition of the Role

The role of the subject coordinator has become firmly established in the primary school in response to many developments in the curriculum since 1989, when the introduction of the National Curriculum in England and Wales began to place countless new pressures on primary school teachers in terms of their subject knowledge and expertise. Teachers were faced with the daunting task of developing quickly their under-standing and capabilities across a broad range of subjects; the response by the majority of schools was to appoint curriculum coordinators for specific curriculum areas and subjects. It is expected that the recent developments in the Foundation Stage may have a similar impact on teachers and practi-tioners of the three to five years' age range, with adults working within these settings taking on the role of coordinator for a specific Early Learning Goal.

The appointment of subject coordinators in educa-tional settings was initiated so that schools and nurseries could capitalize upon the collective subject strengths of the staff, and use this to move forward the teaching and learning in all subjects (Alexander *et al.* 1992). Subject coordination is thus about manag-ing an area of the curriculum to raise standards within the subject and within the context of the school's improvement plan. The subject coordinator achieves this through having a positive influence on their colleagues, children, the headteacher, other adults in the classroom, governors and parents. Effective coordination is therefore only possible where there is a whole school ethos of colleagues supporting colleagues: coordination, although a key feature of the modern school, can only raise standards if all teachers collaborate together and support the subject coordinator. Each subject coordinator cannot be the ultimate expert, particularly when first taking on the role, and so the support of other staff is imperative for a whole-school approach to subject coordination. The headteacher clearly has a role to play in developing and maintaining this ethos and in ensuring consistency of approach, and is thus responsible to the subject coordinator, and must be clear about both the extent of the role within a particular school and the amount of support that is needed by each subject coordinator.

The notion of a subject curriculum coordinator was not entirely new in 1989, but it had previously represented a much smaller, more informal role (Smith 2002). However, the introduction of the National Curriculum led to the role becoming firmly established, and schools began to agree on the responsibilities of the subject coordinator. Coordination posts until that time had been viewed as rewards for general competence that had resulted from long service and experience; the changes in the curriculum brought about a more precise definition of the role. Subject coordinators became no longer responsible merely for making suggestions about topic areas and relevant activities, but were expected to lead the development of the subject throughout their school. Subject coordinators today have responsibility for managing their subject and driving it forward in all areas. This modern role involves:

- Working with staff – to guide and motivate their teaching

- Understanding the subject – what is involved, how to teach it, how it can contribute to the whole school curriculum and how it contributes to the overall education and achievement of all children

- Monitoring and evaluating the effectiveness of teaching and learning

- Identifying needs within the subject and matching them to those of the whole school

- Setting appropriate targets – appropriate to the school improvement plan and thus to school priorities   (Smith 2002)

Prior to 1989, training for the role of subject coordinator had often been unavailable or inadequate; now, some preparation for it is provided during teacher training (Initial Teacher Training), as many newly qualified teachers may take on this increasingly complex and accountable role very early on in their careers. However, in small schools, teaching staff are often required to take the lead in more than one subject area, or staff may be asked to take on the coordination of a subject area in which they have only minimal subject experience. By moving towards a definition of the role of the subject coordinator, the inexperienced or less confident coordinator may begin to better understand the nature and requirements of the position, and also determine their own needs with respect to the responsibility.

The role of the subject coordinator differs markedly from that of a classroom teacher alone, in that the coordinator must develop an overview of a named subject within the school and be responsible for all areas of its management. To do this effectively requires the coordinator to develop a number of skills – to be able to work well with others, to lead by example, to have an understanding of interpersonal relationships, to work as a team or group and to have an adequate knowledge of the subject. The coordinator hence needs a good knowledge of the subject content, an understanding of National Curriculum and/or Early Learning Goals documentation and requirements of the subject, knowledge of how to apply subject knowledge to curriculum requirements and an understanding of how the subject is to be taught most effectively. Quite a tall order!

For the newly appointed coordinator this may appear to be a very intimidating list of requirements, and so in the early stages of holding the position it is important to try and identify immediate priorities for the role and to work purposefully towards them. Support will be available within the school and so a good starting point is to enlist the help of colleagues who are supportive yet constructively critical. Perhaps the most daunting aspect of the role initially is the necessity to lead the development in the subject with staff who may be much more experienced than the coordinator. It is therefore essential to build up the skills needed to work with other staff, particularly those members who are less supportive or less confident, and it is by working alongside the more experienced and supportive staff that the newly appointed coordinator is able to build up his or her own confidence in working with others and in developing *presence* as the subject leader. As the confidence and skills of the coordinator develop, the implementation of the role will widen to include working effectively with all staff in supporting and developing the teaching and learning of the subject being coordinated.

Titles for the role of curriculum coordinator vary within different schools. There may be reference not only to curriculum coordinator but to post holder, subject manager or subject leader; for the purposes of this book the term 'subject coordinator' is used to encompass all these titles (although Chapter 3 looks at the wider implications of the various titles). Whatever title is used, the initial definition of the role indicates a position with managerial demands, a responsibility that is diverse and complex, and within which relationships are central to the effectiveness of the role.

The subject coordinator thus fulfils the roles of educator, adviser and manager. In terms of being an educator, the coordinator aids his or her colleagues in developing their own subject knowledge and under-standing; as adviser, the subject coordinator advises on a range of issues relating to the subject; and the managerial aspect involves creating an ethos for curriculum development and change within the subject (Bentley & Watts 1994). Schools may set out these roles and responsibilities in a variety of ways. They may be issued as part of the job description for a new appointment or as a written list of responsibilities, together with a curriculum plan for the subject. Here are some examples:

Nursery/Infant/Junior School

Job description: Class teacher/Science Coordinator, MPS

General duties

Class teacher for a Year 6 class. This responsibility includes:

- The planning, preparation, delivery and assessment of a varied and relevant curriculum;
- Ensuring a stimulating, active learning environment for pupils through good classroom organization and display;
- Motivating children by personal influence and by awareness of needs; and
- To work as part of the staff team, adhering to the school's behaviour policy, showing consideration to colleagues, assisting in curriculum development, and involvement in extra curricular activities.

Specific responsibilities

- To be responsible for the development of the science curriculum across the school to ensure breadth and balance, progression and continuity.

- To develop and maintain the science policy, guidelines and schemes of work.

- To keep up to date with local and national developments in the science curriculum.

- To liaise where appropriate with other curriculum coordinators.

- To lead staff development in science.

- To support teaching and learning in science across the school.

- To be responsible for monitoring and purchasing resources for science across the school.

Nursery/Infant/Junior School

Curriculum Coordinator responsibilities

- To be responsible for the effective running of the subject within a Key Stage.

- To be responsible for Policy discussions.

- To provide explanation and practical application of subject.

- To liaise with Key staff – the Head, Deputy Head, Key Stage and Year Group Coordinators.

- To support colleagues in meeting the requirements of an effective class teacher.

Successful Subject Co-ordination

- ◆ To provide a good model of practice in line with school policy.

- ◆ To monitor class practice of the subject by developing good working relationships, being positive, and anticipating and resolving problems.

- ◆ To bring issues of concern to the attention of the Senior Management team.

- ◆ To evaluate the implementation of policy and practice.

- ◆ To know the aims of the School Improvement Plan with respect to the subject.

- ◆ To play an active part in the Performance Management System of the school.

- ◆ To be part of the School Management structure.

- ◆ To promote a positive approach and keep abreast of modern education practice.

- ◆ To respect confidentiality at all times.

Nursery/Infant/Junior School

Plan for a Curriculum Area

- ◆ Rationale for the subject in school.

- ◆ Policy for delivery of subject.

- ◆ Scheme of Work for coverage of subject.

- Organization of subject.

- Progression through school.

- Differentiation.

- Special needs provision.

- Health and Safety issues.

- Resources.

- Assessment, Recording and Record-Keeping.

- Portfolio of Moderated work.

The Subject Coordinator will have a clear overview of the subject in school. He/she will also have a clear plan for how the subject is to move forward.

Whatever the format of the school documentation, it is the starting point for the new coordinator, providing the school's interpretation of the role and setting out the responsibilities of the coordinator. Although the role may be redefined in due course, it is this documentation that allows the newly-appointed coordinator to begin developing their effective coordination of the subject. Effective coordination is that which results in well-planned teaching which is organized and delivered appropriately. This enables children to demonstrate improvements in understanding and exhibit progress in relation to previous attainment and, together with their teachers, to display an enthusiasm and interest in the subject. These are the aims of the effective subject coordinator.

2

Getting Started

Getting started as a subject coordinator involves discovering what the school expects from the subject coordinator, what is needed in school to move the subject on – in terms of teaching, learning and achievement by the children, and the needs of the staff in developing their skills and knowledge – and what knowledge, skills and understandings the coordinator needs. This requires an audit of the three areas and the formulation of action plans: an action plan for the development of the subject and an action plan for the development of the coordinator. Action plans are working documents to be added to, amended and referred to at all times. Their formulation at this stage therefore provides a good starting point for discussion with senior management about how the role may be carried out and what may be the training needs of the subject coordinator. Following such a discussion, and any resulting amendments, the action plans thus form the basis of the coordinator's work in school in the early stages of coordination. The checklist below summarizes the action needed at this early stage by the subject coordinator:

✓ Audit the teaching, learning and coordination of the subject

Successful Subject Co-ordination

✓ Identify what *you* want to achieve as the subject coordinator

✓ Audit your own abilities

✓ Consider your own training needs

✓ Commit your ideas to paper

✓ Consider what is essential and what is desirable

✓ Formulate the Coordinator's Action Plans

✓ Break your ideas down into daily, weekly and termly action plans

✓ Share your ideas and action plans with key staff

✓ Identify what parts of the action plan you must carry out and with what parts others can help

✓ Identify the amount of time you are able to give to the role and how this time can be used most effectively

✓ Identify timescales and reviews of progress

It is important that newly appointed coordinators are able to prioritize both their own needs and those of the school in order to produce good quality, appropriate action plans. Trying to do too much too soon is as ineffective as trying to do too little. The new coordinator may consider the vastness of the task requires everything to be addressed at once, or may consider it too daunting and not know where to begin! The action plans therefore enable the new subject coordinator to prioritize the action to be taken; by considering the needs of the school first, the coordinator will be able to identify the skills and knowledge needed to begin to fulfil the role of subject coordinator.

An audit of the subject within school is in itself quite a time-consuming process, and yet it is extremely important to the development of effective coordination. The subject coordinator must have a good overview of the current state of the subject in school in order to establish where the school is now, where it needs to be and how it is going to get there. It necessitates a review of the subject curriculum, the school's aims and objectives for the subject and how the subject is taught in school. There are various sources of information that can be used:

✓ The current school policy for the subject

✓ The current Scheme of Work for the subject

✓ Other school documentation for the subject

✓ LEA guidelines for the subject

✓ The School Improvement Plan

✓ Ofsted comments regarding the subject

✓ Talking to colleagues

✓ Talking to children

✓ Observations of displayed work

Although the monitoring and evaluation of lessons will give an excellent *feel* for the subject and how it is taught, the coordinator may not be involved in these activities during the early stages of coordination, and so an action plan may be formulated purely from the information gained through audit. The focus for the action plan will be on improving the quality of teaching and learning within the subject: all other points in the action plan are to support this, and so the coordinator must be mindful of the needs of the children and the qualifications and experience of the staff when formulating the plan. A further aspect to consider at this stage is the facilities, equipment and resources available.

One final consideration before the coordinator is able to prepare the action plan is the time available to put the plan into force, as there is no point in devising an extensive plan that requires a huge time input when time is clearly limited. It must be remembered that the coordinator will also have classroom responsibilities as a class teacher, and may be required to coordinate another subject or subjects. There may be little or no non-contact time available during the school day and so the coordinator must be able to target the areas of coordination most in need of development. An action plan is therefore essential for the new subject coordinator to indicate clearly how the coordinator is to begin to manage the subject.

Following the audit of the subject in school, the coordinator therefore devises an action plan setting out how the subject is to move forward. Action plans take various forms; but many schools use a standard format. The checklist below summarizes the information to be included in the subject coordinator's action plan:

✓ Strengths and weaknesses of the subject

✓ Evidence for the judgements

✓ Priorities for development

✓ Action to be taken

✓ Criteria for achievement of the development

✓ Evaluation of the action taken

The formulation of the action plan will then aid the coordinator in prioritizing his or her own training needs. It can be appreciated that there are a range of skills needed by the coordinator, together with the need to develop a good knowledge and understanding of the subject. By matching his or her own needs to the needs of the subject action plan, the coordinator is able both to plan personal development as a coordinator at a suitable pace and to support the needs of the school. A consideration of the types of activity the subject coordinator may expect to be involved in will aid in finalizing both the subject action plan and his or her personal action plan. The checklist below summarizes some of the main activities of the effective subject coordinator:

✓ Maintaining a clear overview of the subject in school

✓ Maintaining the impact of the subject

✓ Providing a rationale for the subject

✓ Facilitating reviews of policy and practice

✓ Providing guidelines for the organization of the subject

✓ Producing associated documentation – a policy for the delivery of the subject and a Scheme of

Successful Subject Co-ordination

Work for coverage and progression through school

✓ Providing guidelines on differentiation, Special Educational Needs provision and Health and Safety issues

✓ Liasing with other subject coordinators in the school

✓ Maintaining dialogue with the Head and the Senior Management Team

✓ Advising on the practical application of the subject

✓ Supporting teaching and learning across the school

✓ Demonstrating a good model of practice

✓ Leading staff development

✓ Developing a range of good working relationships

✓ Developing the use of assessment, recording and record-keeping

✓ Improving attainment within the subject

✓ Monitoring teaching and learning of the subject in school

✓ Ensuring that the subject is well resourced

✓ Purchasing, organizing and evaluating good quality, child-appropriate resources

✓ Keeping up to date with local and national developments in the subject

✓ Ensuring the subject continues to be represented well within the school's curriculum

This checklist clearly expresses the range and complexity of the role of the subject coordinator, and the range of knowledge, skills and understandings it demands can thus be appreciated. These will be discussed in later chapters: however, at this early stage, a key skill to be developed, alongside that of time management, is organization. Indeed, within this section it has been demonstrated how much paperwork is to be accessed and used by the coordinator: and many subject coordinators deal with this requirement to work with paperwork, and to generate their own paperwork, by developing a good filing system. Documents used are kept for reference within a box or filing cabinet and a record of work kept in a subject coordinator's file. This file serves many purposes – it forms a record of work carried out, it is a reference document, it is a working document for the coordinator to use and may be used for Performance Management purposes or as evidence towards the National Standards for subject leaders (this is covered in Chapter 3). The file is therefore a necessity and one that can be started as soon as the coordinator is appointed. The organization and contents of the file and the associated box of documentation are totally at the discretion of the subject coordinator; the checklists below suggest what the effective subject coordinator may include.

The subject coordinator's file may include:

✓ A policy statement for the subject

Successful Subject Co-ordination

✓ Job description or list of coordinator responsibilities

✓ Curriculum plan

✓ School test data and current targets

✓ Names of contacts, e.g. other coordinators, Local Education Authority advisers

✓ Subject audit

✓ Coordinator's action plan

✓ Action plan reviews

✓ Record of work carried out

✓ Notes on special events

✓ Record of monitoring and evaluation activities – including release time, classroom observations, assessing work, displays, etc.

✓ Record of all meetings

The subject coordinator's box of documentation may include:

✓ The current policy for the subject

✓ The current Scheme of Work

✓ LEA guidelines for the subject

✓ Current Ofsted report

✓ Other school documentation related to the subject

✓ A bank of ideas for educational visits related to the subject

✓ In-Service log – school INSET planned and delivered, external courses attended and reviews of INSET courses attended

✓ School planning for the subject – copies of year group medium- and short-term planning

✓ Work samples and photographs

✓ Assessed work

✓ Relevant books, references, newspaper articles, etc.

✓ Resource log – list of current resources, copies of all resource orders

The formulation of the action plans, the collection of associated documentation and starting the co-ordinator's file are crucial first steps in taking charge of the role of the subject coordinator and in tailoring it to the needs both of the school and the coordinator. It must also be remembered that it is essential for the coordinator to keep the headteacher, the senior management team and the governors up to date with both the work being carried out in the subject and the work intended to be carried out, and the sharing of the action plans and the coordinator's file are good starting points for this dialogue. Indeed, another essential skill for the coordinator is that of communication as two of the main responsibilities of the subject coordinator are to ensure that all adults connected with the school are aware of developments in the subject and that the developments are grounded in the school's policies and practices. The many facets of communication are considered in more detail in Chapter 5.

3

Subject Coordinator or Subject Leader?

The title 'subject coordinator' is being used throughout the book, and yet it is accepted that the role has gone beyond that of simply coordinating activities and resources. The main difference now is that the subject coordinator is expected to lead the development of the subject in all areas and the role includes at least some elements of monitoring and evaluating the quality of work in the subject being led and in the strategic planning of the subject. In view of this, the term 'subject coordinator' may be too limited a description for the extent of the work being carried out today. By introducing monitoring and evaluation to the role, it is expanded to become a managerial position and involvement in strategic planning points towards the leadership aspect of the role, as introduced in Chapter 1. In view of this, the title for the subject coordinator may incorporate these require- ments and be more appropriately termed 'subject manager' or 'subject leader', indeed, there are now National Standards for the subject leader, alongside the National Standards for the award of Qualified Teacher Status (QTS), Special Educational Needs Coordinators and Headteachers, establishing the importance of these aspects of the role (TTA 1998). The aims of the National Standards are listed as:

◆ Setting out clear expectations for teachers

◆ Helping teachers to plan and monitor their development, training and performance effectively

◆ Helping teachers to set clear, relevant targets for improving their effectiveness

◆ Ensuring the focus is on improving the achievement of pupils and the quality of their education

◆ Providing a basis for the professional recognition of teachers' expertise and achievements

◆ Helping providers of professional development to plan and provide high quality, relevant training which meets the needs of individual teachers

◆ Making good use of time and having the maximum benefit for pupils

The National Standards specific to subject leaders thus set out the knowledge, understanding, skills and attributes needed for the role and provide an on-going checklist for the coordinator of the types of activity they should be carrying out. In addition, they indicate the direction the professional development of the effective subject coordinator should be taking. The Standards may therefore be used to build upon the initial action plans devised by the coordinator and to develop the coordinator's interpretation of the role towards one inclusive of leadership and management.

The five standards specific to the role of the subject leader are:

1. Core purpose of the subject leader.

2. Key outcomes of subject leadership.

3. Professional knowledge and understanding.

4. Skills and attributes.

5. Key areas of subject leadership.

Within each standard is a comprehensive list of requirements; these are summarized below.

1. *Core purpose of the subject leader*

The core purpose of the subject leader is to provide leadership and management in a subject that ensures high-quality teaching and learning and improved standards of achievement for all pupils. All the information in this book, including the roles and responsibilities already listed, is provided to support this standard.

2. *Key outcomes of subject leadership*

The outcomes include: an improvement in the achievement of children in both the subject area and in literacy, numeracy and information technology skills; the development of teamwork within which the coordinator supports their colleagues in the subject; increased parental understanding; a knowledgeable headteacher and senior management team; and an informed wider community.

3. *Professional knowledge and understanding*

The standards recognize the needs of the subject leader in developing knowledge and understanding that is subject-specific, and in the requirement to keep up to date with developments in their subject area, but list under this standard the knowledge and understanding required for the *leadership* aspect of the role. These relate to knowledge of the school's priorities, the relationship of the subject to the curriculum as whole, statutory requirements for the subject and the assessment, recording and reporting of pupils' attainment and progress. Also included here are the requirements regarding monitoring, evaluation and using inspection evidence and data to set targets for improvement.

4. *Skills and attributes*

These are the leadership skills, attributes and professional competences needed to be able to lead and manage people and teams. They include decision-making skills, communication skills, self-management and personal attributes.

5. *Key areas of subject leadership*

The standards list four key areas of subject leadership: strategic direction and development of the subject; teaching and learning; leading and managing staff; and the efficient and effective deployment of staff and resources. Subject leaders are expected to demonstrate their ability to apply their professional knowledge, understanding, skills and attributes to these key areas.

The standards for the subject leader thus recognize the valuable contribution the role can make to school life as a whole and demonstrate how the role is to be elevated to a position of real responsibility within the school structure. For the newly-appointed subject coordinator the full range of the National Standards may appear unattainable, but the advice contained within this book will enable the first tentative steps into the role, and then develop it into one where all the standards are being met. The newly-appointed subject coordinator will therefore begin the role by concentrating on the immediate needs of the coordination of the subject in school, but will quickly move on to identifying how he or she will both lead and manage the subject effectively. Thus, the title of *subject coordinator* is probably the most appropriate term to use in the beginning stages of the role and so will continue to be used throughout the book to avoid confusion, although the reader will now appreciate the way in which the role has developed and how, as a result, the title used should move from *subject coordinator* to *subject leader*.

In moving forward along this path, the subject coordinator again must consider the time allocation they are to give to the role and to his or her development towards becoming an effective subject leader and manager. The developing role obviously demands day-to-day management of matters relating to the subject, planned action over a term or a year to improve the delivery of the subject in school and a long-term view of where the subject is to be led; the effective subject coordinator must therefore be able to reassess the needs of the role and allocate their time accordingly.

This does not, however, necessarily imply the need for the coordinator to increase the time allocation they give to the role; rather, it suggests that the coordinator must develop the essential skill of time management. The effective subject coordinator must thus recognize the range of activities to be carried out on an informal day-to-day basis (such as resource management and liaison with others about the subject), those activities which need to be planned and formalized (such as supporting staff in their planning and delivery of the subject) and those which are needed to move the subject forward (such as modelling lessons and inspiring innovation in the subject). This, in turn, will require the coordinator to extend the scope of their overview of the subject being led. Within school, this will be more fully achieved through the monitoring and evaluation of lessons (Chapter 6), but the process can begin by simply talking to staff and children about their perceptions of the subject in school but with the use of focused questions to elicit the information the coordinator requires, rather than the informal discussions that took place in the early coordination of the subject.

Looking at planning for the subject will identify how the subject is planned for in each year group and the activities to be carried out. At this stage, the coordinator must develop an understanding of the assessment of the subject, in order to consider the standards of achievement attained by the children. Are the national expected averages for attainment being achieved or exceeded? Reading school documenta-tion will inform the coordinator of the philosophy of the school and its aims and the make up of the whole school curriculum, while focused observations will enable judgements about the policies in practice within the school and their effectiveness in develop-ing teaching and learning within the subject.

Subject Coordinator or Subject Leader?

In order for the role to move towards one of leadership and management, the coordinator must begin to be involved in strategic planning for the subject, both as a stand-alone subject and as part of the school's whole curriculum. This requirement builds on both the knowledge about the subject the coordinator develops (Chapter 4) and the ability to relate this knowledge to the needs of the school and the needs of the children. In practical terms it requires the coordinator to have involvement in the School Improvement Plan, in planning and leading In-service training in the subject and in preparing documentation relating to the subject (Chapter 8). The development of subject-specific knowledge is therefore vital to the development of the role of the subject coordinator.

4

The Expert

One of the keys to being an effective subject coordinator is the development of subject expertise (Alexander *et al*. 1992). This requires the coordinator to acquire an extensive knowledge and understanding of the subject: of the factors that promote effective learning in the subject and of the skills needed to teach the subject successfully. Developing subject expertise can be achieved in a variety of ways: through local school networks, through the Local Education Authority, by accessing relevant websites on the Internet (the DfES standards site, the virtual teachers centre, etc), personal reading, training courses, postgraduate study and by involvement with subject-specific professional bodies. Another important aspect of subject expertise is keeping up to date with current thinking and current trends in the subject. Although subject knowledge is vital, it is knowledge of current ideas surrounding the teaching of the subject, and how these ideas are made relevant to the school setting, which is fundamental to the leadership of the subject in school.

Subject expertise therefore needs to be considered both in terms of the subject within the school, and also the progress of the subject outside school. It is thus one of the central responsibilities of a subject coordinator to extend their subject expertise, as the ability of the coordinator to move a subject forward originates from this knowledge. Accordingly, the coordinator must also possess, or acquire, the skills needed to disseminate such expertise to others within the school, in order to continue to develop quality teaching and learning in the subject across the whole school.

The coordinator may wish to consider first what it is that defines the subject they are coordinating. Each subject can be defined by the subject knowledge that is needed and by the way of working used within it. A subject is therefore not simply 'information' to be imparted: it is knowledge and understanding to be acquired. Each subject thus has a specific structure and often its own language. Subject expertise is consequently much more than a bank of information, it must be thought of as comprising of four, interlinked, components:

- Knowledge of subject content

- Knowledge of National Curriculum requirements, including assessment

- Knowledge of how to apply subject knowledge in teaching pupils

- Knowledge of developments in the subject

There are plenty of sources available to the new coordinator for the development of each strand noted above. Many educational books are now written covering all subjects, of which several are to be found in high street bookshops and are advertised in educational publications. The Internet provides a myriad of information regarding teaching, learning and subject knowledge. Most, if not all, the subject areas have a professional body of which the new coordinator is eligible, for a small fee, to become a member (indeed, many schools pay for school membership of such bodies). Each body provides some or all of the following:

- Newsletters

- Journals

- Advice notes

- Advice help lines

- Local meetings

- Publications

Membership to such professional bodies provides huge support to the subject coordinator at whatever stage they have reached in developing the coordination of the subject being led. The Local Education Authority is also a source of excellent support to the coordinator, through the provision of appropriate training, information and advice, and a library area designated for the subject. The Local Educational Authority and/or the subject professional body may organize local group meetings for coordinators of a specific subject. These are invaluable sources of support for the newly-appointed coordinator, as they provide an arena for much discussion and sharing of ideas. If such a meeting is not available in the local area it is worth considering setting up such a group –

indeed, the Local Educational Authority and/or the professional body may provide help in this, or local schools may be interested in getting together to form a small steering committee.

One of the main challenges facing the subject coordinator is to ensure that the subject retains its status in the school and that sufficient time is given over to its study. This is crucial for the maintenance and development of teaching and learning in the subject. The introduction of the Literacy and Numeracy Strategies into schools has had a profound impact on the status of other subjects in the curriculum, and an inevitable influence on the time allocated to all subjects. Similarly, parallel changes to the priorities for initial teacher training are also likely to impact upon the preparedness of some newly-qualified teachers to deliver quality teaching in all subjects in the primary curriculum. The introduction of the Early Learning Goals for the Foundation Stage have added a further need to develop progression and continuity in the range of subjects, and yet the existence of national documentation alone cannot ensure quality teaching and learning and the adequate and effective coverage of each subject area.

The role of the subject coordinator is thus to ensure that teaching and learning within the subject in the school is effective and that the coverage of the subject is sufficient to improve the attainment of children. The effective subject coordinator is able to promote the development of the subject through monitoring and evaluating teaching, working alongside colleagues in their planning and delivery of the subject, providing demonstration lessons and suggesting innovative approaches to learning and conducting curriculum development through meetings and In-service. The need for subject expertise has never been greater, in order to allow the coordinator to effectively carry out these leadership and management activities for the subject they are coordinating.

It can thus be appreciated that although the acquisition of subject expertise is vital to the effective coordination of a subject, it is also vital that the coordinator is able to use such expertise in the school setting. The need to secure and sustain effective teaching of the subject by all members of staff is another key requirement of the coordinator and necessitates the coordinator being able to disseminate good practice within the school (Chapters 5 and 8). In order to carry out this important role, the coordinator must develop an understanding of what constitutes good practice in the subject, both in the classroom and across the whole school. Sources of support for the subject coordinator in developing his or her understanding of good practice include those already noted, together with guidance from Ofsted (Chapter 7). Good practice within the classroom setting is considered in Chapter 6: the checklist below provides an overview of the requirements of good practice across a key stage or a whole school:

✓ Full subject coverage across a key stage

✓ A clear sequence of objectives and activities

✓ Continuity and progression in the subject across and between key stages

✓ Differentiated teaching to cater for all needs,

including children of high ability, children with special educational needs, and children with linguistic needs

✓ Clear expectations for teaching and learning in the subject, consistently applied by all teaching staff

✓ Assessment-led planning

✓ A clear policy for assessment, recording and reporting of the subject

✓ The use of a range of appropriate teaching and learning methods

✓ The promotion through the subject of literacy, numeracy and information technology skills

✓ Use of assessments and local and national data to set targets for further improvement

✓ The transfer of information regarding teaching and learning in the subject from the leaving teacher to the receiving teacher and from one key stage to the next

✓ Regular monitoring and evaluation of subject lessons

✓ Curriculum evaluation of the subject that identifies effective practice and areas for improvement

✓ Effective sharing of expertise between staff

✓ Effective sharing of information about the subject with governors, parents and the local community

This checklist provides the subject coordinator with a basis for further development both of the subject in school and of their role within it. It can be appreciated that effective subject coordination requires a continuous cycle of auditing the effectiveness of the curriculum provision for the subject, followed by the setting in place of appropriate action to improve practice, then evaluation of the action leading to a further audit. Alongside this is the need for the coordinator to develop the knowledge, skills and understandings necessary to deliver the cycle of improvements. In addition to this is the need to keep up to date with developments in the subject outside the school setting, and to relate these to the school setting. Again, quite a tall order for the subject coordinator who is also a full-time class teacher! But it must be remembered that the coordination of a subject and the development of subject expertise are on-going processes that will continue throughout the teacher's career.

The listed requirements look unattainable, indeed they would be if they were to be carried out at the same time, and so the newly appointed subject coordinator needs to identify a starting point for the development of his or her subject expertise. This starting point must always be based on what expertise the coordinator already has, matched to what is needed to deliver the subject action plan, thereby beginning the process of moving the subject forward through effective coordination. The checklist below will help the newly appointed subject coordinator to identify where to begin the process of developing subject expertise:

✓ Review the subject action plan

✓ Identify the requirements of each stage of the

action plan

✓ Ensure each stage supports the development of teaching and learning within the subject

✓ Identify the knowledge, skills and understandings needed by the coordinator in order to put the action into place

✓ Consider what knowledge, skills and understandings you already have and what you need to acquire

✓ Identify the sources of support to develop these aspects of subject expertise

✓ Develop a training plan setting out how the knowledge, skills and understandings will be developed, including timescales and criteria for success

✓ Share the training plan with key staff in school, including the Head

This checklist will aid the coordinator in committing his or her ideas to paper and in prioritizing what is needed. It will also ensure that the coordinator's training plan is matched both to the development of quality of teaching and learning in the subject, and to the improved attainment of children in the subject, therefore enabling the new coordinator to begin purposeful work in the coordination of the subject.

An important inclusion in the training plan will be training in the skills needed to work with staff in a variety of situations: on a one-to-one basis, in small groups and with the whole staff. The coordinator will necessarily work with a range of adults and must therefore develop the skills to interact with others in whatever capacity is required. It must be remembered that the basic requirements of the subject coordinator role today are the provision of leadership and direction for their subject, and the need to ensure that the subject is managed and organized to meet the aims and objectives of the school. This indicates strongly the need for the subject coordinator to be fully involved in all aspects of the subject, including the strategic planning of the subject in school, and so it is vitally important that the coordinator develops a range of interpersonal skills and is able to communicate well with all adults in school (Jenkins *et al*. 2000).

5

Working with Staff

Working with staff in the school as the subject coordinator is probably the most important aspect of the coordinator's role. The coordinator can only promote quality teaching and learning in the subject, and thus improved attainment by the children, through working with staff. The coordinator cannot effect improvements within the subject without the support and cooperation of the staff – indeed, there is no point in the coordinator developing subject expertise if it cannot be disseminated and used through the school. However, working with staff is a huge area to consider and demands the use of many skills. It covers many situations, from simply being available to offer informal support for colleagues through to being available for staff to confide in, to planning and delivering In-service and to leading the staff through curriculum change. The range of activities includes:

♦ Informal, one-to-one discussions about an aspect of the subject

♦ Informal, small group discussions about an aspect of the subject

♦ Meetings with the Head and senior management team

Successful Subject Co-ordination

- Meetings with the governors

- Presenting information to staff, parents and governors

- Staff meetings to introduce new ideas and guidelines

- Working alongside staff to develop policies and practice

- Working with staff on planning and assessment issues

- Liaising with staff on a range of curriculum issues

- Working in the classroom – monitoring and evaluating the work of staff, shared teaching, modelling lessons for staff

- Working with staff in a variety of situations to implement change

Working with staff will begin when the subject coordinator is newly appointed, probably even before the coordinator has started their audit of the subject and their consideration of the action plans! It is a feature of the modern school that many teachers now expect to consult a subject coordinator for help and advice and, in return, expect support from the coordinator. Even if the coordinator is also a newly qualified teacher, there will be an expectation that advice and suggestions will be forthcoming! It is important therefore that the subject coordinator is ready to offer informal advice and support from day one of their coordination of the subject. However, staff generally recognize that the coordinator cannot know everything about the subject being led, and so being approachable is much, more important than having a bank of knowledge that other staff cannot share. Indeed, the subject coordinator who is able to show support by empathizing with individual members of staff and assisting them in finding out the information they require will be one of the most effective subject leaders.

Informal guidance and support may be needed across a range of issues related to teaching and learning, including planning, delivery, assessment and subject knowledge, and so it is clear that the development of subject expertise is necessary for these day-to-day interactions. However, although the need to be available for informal support and guidance will remain an on-going aspect of the role of the subject coordinator, in order to effectively carry out the leadership and management of the subject more formal means of support and guidance will need to be planned. It must also be remembered that whatever means the coordinator is using to support staff, it is the striving to move the subject forward that is most important, and so the effective subject coordinator will use all opportunities for staff interaction to introduce good practice into the subject teaching.

In addition to providing guidance and support, it can be appreciated that the role of the coordinator involves the planning and delivery of subject-specific training to the staff. Training for staff may be needed in:

◆ Subject-specific knowledge

Successful Subject Co-ordination

- Approaches to teaching
- Approaches to learning
- Assessing outcomes

The coordinator must therefore have the ability to plan and deliver training that is relevant to the subject being led, to the school setting and to the needs of the staff. Such training may challenge the staff and their ways of thinking about the subject and their teaching; consequently, the coordinator must be sympathetic to the current curricular demands of the school and the abilities of the staff, in order to plan and deliver training that sustains motivation for the subject and its development in school. This requires great sensitivity and a range of skills (indeed, the notion of the development of relevant skills has been noted throughout this book).

The development of skills must feature in the coordinator's training plan. Skills are developed through observing others and trying out their methods of skill development and management. The coordinator may therefore return to the small group of supportive yet critical teachers whose help was enlisted in the early stages of coordination. This group will be invaluable in offering suggestions in skill management, in enabling the coordinator to try out his or her developing skills and in evaluating the success of the coordinator in developing the skills needed to carry out the role. However, the range of skills needed by the subject coordinator is almost endless! For the individual coordinator the list must include personal and interpersonal skills that are matched to both the role of the coordinator and to the needs of the school. Therefore, it is pertinent to consider the skills needed by the effective subject coordinator under broad headings. The checklist below presents some of these headings, and thus the main skills, the coordinator needs to develop:

- ✓ Time management
- ✓ Organization
- ✓ Planning
- ✓ Problem-solving
- ✓ Evaluation
- ✓ Reflection
- ✓ Communication
- ✓ Motivation
- ✓ Teamwork and team building
- ✓ Leadership

It can be appreciated that the headings used in the first part of the list are personal skills and attributes needed by the coordinator, while the headings listed further down are the necessary inter-personal skills needed by the coordinator.

Personal skills

Although listed as independent skills, the personal skills and attributes required by the effective subject coordinator are inter-related. It can be appreciated that the effective coordinator must be able to organize his or her time well. The need to balance the workload of a successful class teacher with that of a subject leader cannot be understated. The formulation of good action plans that are subject to on-going referral is the starting point for good time management, leading to achievement of the balance needed between the roles of class teacher and subject leader. Throughout the book, the need to reassess the time commitment to the coordination of the subject has been stated, together with the need to consider the relevance of the action plans to the necessary developments in the subject being led. There are many strategies to aid the coordinator in time-management: one of which is to develop organizational skills.

It has been demonstrated above that the successful coordination of a subject is a complex task that requires a range of knowledge, skills and understandings. The coordinator will carry out a myriad of activities related to developing teaching and learning within the subject. In addition to this the coordinator will be managing his or her own training and dealing with a wealth of paperwork. The need to be organized is therefore essential to the task. Beginning a filing system for documentation and recording the work carried out by the coordinator is an excellent start – but organization is about much more than this. It is about prioritizing needs within the coordination of the subject – the needs of the coordinator, the needs of the school and the needs of the staff – and detailing the action to be taken in response to these needs. It is therefore about setting realistic goals to be met within a certain time frame. From this can be acknowledged how the skills of time management and organization are related; being organized ensures the coordinator uses his or her time appropriately, and being able to use time appropriately to set, and meet, short-term goals aids the coordinator in his or her organization.

Planning skills and problem-solving skills are also necessary for the effective subject coordinator and, moreover, contribute to his or her skills of organization and time management. The coordinator will clearly using planning skills in a variety of contexts – action planning, planning lessons, planning meetings and planning In-service – to name but a few, all of which involve problem solving. The ability to plan well includes the need to choose a suitable format for the plans to be committed to paper, to consider the relevance of the planning to the context and to visualize the plans in practice. The range of skills used in planning and problem solving are numerous, for example, reviewing current practice, matching current practice to needs, identifying relevant priorities, turning relevant priorities into action to be taken … they are therefore again almost impossible to list. Consequently, it can be seen why the range of skills needed by the effective subject coordinator is being considered under such broad headings as 'planning' and 'problem solving'.

Following the planning and implementation of action related to the role of the subject coordinator, the processes of evaluation and reflection are needed. These aid the coordinator in judging his or her own effectiveness and the effectiveness of the work being carried out. However, the coordinator must develop the skills necessary to achieve an objective evaluation and reflection of the coordination of the subject. Thus the coordinator must be able to identify strengths and weaknesses, and be able to use these judgements when planning further action. Seeking the opinions of colleagues is part of this process, as their comments will provide relevant information regarding the coordinator's performance and the advances made towards meeting the objectives set out in the action plan. Using these skills will support the on-going cycle of development in the subject: the cycle of reviewing, action planning, action implementation, followed by evaluation and reflection, and then reviewing once more.

Interpersonal skills

Under the broad headings listed earlier are the four most important inter-personal skills needed by the effective subject coordinator: communication, motivation, teamwork and team building, and leadership. Again these are clearly linked, however, by far the main skill needed by the successful coordinator is that of communication. Indeed, it is imperative that the coordinator is able to communicate effectively with staff both collectively and on a one-to-one basis. It may be assumed that all teachers are natural communicators, as much of the teacher's role involves communicating with others, and thus that communication with other staff will be a matter of course: however, this is not always so when transferring the skills of the teacher to the role of the subject coordinator. It must be remembered that communication may take many forms and involves many skills; it is not just about speaking to others but involves listening, empathizing, responding appropriately and considering the needs of who is being communicated with. Communication is also concerned with non-verbal gestures and with written forms of communication. It can thus be appreciated that there are many considerations involved with communication, and possibly many new skills to be learned.

The subject coordinator will use communication in both formal and informal settings. Verbal communication must allow for the coordinator to listen as well as speak, to ensure both participants feel involved and are able both to check that each understands the other, and to share an agreed view of what has been communicated. Verbal communication is a valuable strategy for coordinators as it can be used for many purposes – praise, recognition, information, messages, and so on. It is also valuable in that coordinators will receive instant feedback – either verbal or non-verbal – on their own performance and effectiveness. Both participants in the communication will be mindful of the non-verbal elements of the communication – the body language – and the tone in which the communication was delivered. These are equally as important as the content of the communication.

A major disadvantage of verbal communication is that it may easily be forgotten or remembered inaccurately, and may need to be repeated or reinforced. It then becomes important again that the coordinator ensures there is a shared understanding about what has been said. When planning verbal communications it is necessary to consider the timing and the setting, as these are crucial to its effectiveness. All participants must have the time for, and feel comfortable about, listening to the coordinator, asking questions and accepting the appropriate responses. They must be able to focus without being distracted by what is happening around them.

Written communication skills are also essential for the coordinator as it is not always possible, or appropriate, to engage in verbal communication with all members of staff. This may be due to time constraints or because written communication is a preferred method of information transfer. However, as with verbal communication, there are many factors to consider. It is vitally important that the communication is actually needed! This may seem an obvious requirement, but consideration must be given to the wealth of information in paper form teachers now receive, and so the coordinator must consider whether another piece of paper is warranted, or if verbal communication would be the preferred method of communication.

Unlike verbal communication, written communication does not allow for two-way conversation and so does not permit questioning or clarification of the information. Following a consideration of the advantages and disadvantages of written communication, if it is deemed appropriate, then the coordinator must be able to plan the written communication well. This includes the content of the communication, its presentation and the language used. The coordinator must decide on the tone, the choice of words – to ensure there is no ambiguity in the information communicated – and the relevance to the audience. Care needs to be given to the presentation in order to interest the reader, for example, use of bullet points, note form or short sentences. It can thus be appreciated yet again that the skills involved in communication are numerous but vital to the successful coordination of the subject. The coordinator will have many models in school of good communicators, and this will be of use in developing this essential skill.

One of the major threats to the development of any subject in school is motivation or, more correctly, lack of motivation. Motivation is needed to carry through any action led by the coordinator, and so the coordinator must be able to motivate and inspire their colleagues. There are many motivational techniques to be learned, including communicating with staff in such a way that the action proposed is deemed to be relevant to their needs and that it will be implemented in an appropriate manner. Above all, coordinators must display their own motivation for the subject and for the developments taking place within it. Coordinators must also be able to detect a lack of motivation, or deterioration in motivation for the subject. This may be demonstrated through absence from meetings, lack of punctuality at meetings, avoidance of the coordinator or poor performance in teaching. The coordinator may thus need to work individually with the member of staff to raise or regain motivation, by leading through example or providing individualized help.

Successful Subject Co-ordination

The skills of teamwork, team building and leadership are all related to motivation for the subject. The coordinator must be able to develop a team approach to the planning and delivery of the subject, to ensure the action planned is implemented and leads to improvements in teaching, learning and attainment. Using the team approach thus ensures staff involvement, support and active participation in the subject, and gives credit to the efforts of others. However, it is still the responsibility of the coordinator to lead the subject and to provide guidance and support to the staff, in order to move the subject forward in school. This requires the coordinator to use all the personal and inter-personal skills already discussed.

The range of activities within which the subject coordinator will be working with staff is again almost endless! A definitive list would be nearly impossible to compile: however, some of the activities will be considered in detail in later sections. The skills and attributes that the coordinator is able to develop support this most rewarding aspect of the role, not only in terms of improving teaching and learning of the subject within school, but also in terms of working with fellow professionals. Gone are the days when teachers worked in almost isolation from other teachers: today's teaching is much more about teamwork, and the part played in this by the effective subject leader cannot be understated.

6

Monitoring and Evaluation

Monitoring and evaluation are the most recent responsibilities to be added to the role of subject coordinator and are what changes the role from one of coordination to one of leadership and management. Monitoring is the process of checking what is happening and the extent to which teaching and learning have gone to plan; evaluation is the collection, analysis, discussion and reporting of evidence that allows judgements to be made about whether or not we are being successful (Jenkins *et al.* 2000). It indicates the standards of teaching and learning in the subject and determines if these are good enough within the school context, and thus whether to consolidate the teaching approaches and learning outcomes or to implement changes. Evaluation considers the achievements of children and indicates whether the progress made is good enough. The processes therefore contribute to the accountability and development of the curriculum as a whole; accountability is what demonstrates a commitment to maintaining and improving standards. The processes of monitoring and evaluation thus provide data and evidence that feeds into the cycle of continuous improvement, and are critical tools in developing and maintaining effective teaching and learning in the classroom, by accurately identifying what is currently being planned, delivered and achieved within the subject.

When carrying out monitoring and evaluation there are six questions to consider:

◆ What is to be monitored and evaluated?

◆ How is the monitoring and evaluation to be carried out?

◆ Where is the monitoring and evaluation to be carried out?

◆ How often will the monitoring and evaluation be carried out?

◆ When will the monitoring and evaluation be carried out?

◆ How will the results of monitoring and evaluation be used to improve teaching and learning?

(Singleton 2000)

Monitoring and evaluation should cover all aspects of the subject, encompassing the curriculum planning, delivery and outcomes. This necessitates the monitoring and evaluation of the planning for the subject, the teaching of the subject, the learning within the subject and the attainment of the children. The outcomes will indicate the relevance of the school's Scheme of Work to each year group, the suitability of planned activities to each year group and the effectiveness of the teaching methods used. There are various contexts for carrying out monitoring and evaluation activities related to each of these areas; these will be discussed in some detail later in this Chapter.

Monitoring and evaluation takes place throughout school and beyond, during the school day and outside the school day. It includes activities inside the classroom such as lesson observations and the scrutiny of children's work, around school when observing corridor displays and discussing the subject with children, and beyond the school day during meetings, In-service and assessment meetings with colleagues in school or colleagues from other schools. It is important that monitoring and evaluating all aspects of the subject are established as on-going processes that are part of the improvement cycle. Informal monitoring and evaluation may take place on a daily basis; it is the planned monitoring and evaluation activities that the coordinator will use to move the subject forward most effectively. A planned monitoring and evaluation activity is thus a formal process and it is at the school's discretion how often such activities are carried out. The checklist below provides a summary of time scales for planned monitoring and evaluation activities:

✓ Daily – through teacher's self-reviews and informal observations

✓ Weekly – by year group staff

✓ End of unit/termly – by year group staff, the scrutiny of medium-/short-term planning, assessment conferences and formal observation

✓ Annually – through attainment and target setting, optional and statutory SATs

✓ At other times (formally, as negotiated) as part of a subject coordinator's plan, through concerns raised, performance management, requirements of the SDP or Ofsted action plan

(Singleton 2000)

It must be remembered that monitoring involves overseeing what is planned in teaching, what is delivered and what is received; evaluation then takes the results and matches them to the expectations of the school. The results of monitoring and evaluation therefore identify the strengths and weaknesses of the current provision for the subject. Where concerns are raised the headteacher and the senior management team must be informed and decisions made to remedy them. This may result in advice to the teachers involved, improvements made to the Scheme of Work or even change to the requirements for the subject in school. Where particular concerns are not raised, the outcomes of the monitoring and evaluation activity are compared to what the school has identified is to be achieved, particularly with respect to teaching and learning and the targets that have been set, and will indicate either change, if needed, or maintenance of the curriculum. The stages following monitoring and evaluation are therefore to:

- Identify changes needed (if any) to the provision for the subject

- Identify training needs

- Identify support needs

- Formulate an INSET plan

- Identify future targets

- Use the data to inform the school improvement plan

- Share results – with staff through staff meetings, review reports and/or summaries and the governing body through the individual subject governor and/or the School Improvement Plan

(Singleton 2000)

Monitoring and evaluation are thus very important responsibilities for the subject coordinator and again require the development and use of subject expertise. In order to carry out monitoring and evaluation activities the coordinator must have a view of what constitutes good practice in the subject while remaining open to innovative and new teaching approaches. He or she must have an understanding of age-appropriate attainment within the subject and possess sound subject knowledge. The coordinator must also have the skills necessary for working alongside staff in the classroom and for making judgments about the planning and delivery of the subject being led. However, monitoring and evaluation through observing lessons is only one aspect of the processes. The checklist below provides the coordinator with a range of other monitoring and evaluation activities which may be used:

✓ The scrutiny of planning – both medium- and short-term plans

✓ Discussion with pupils

Successful Subject Co-ordination

✓ The scrutiny of pupils' work (during moderation meetings)

✓ SATs analyses

✓ The analysis of assessment/target setting information

✓ Discussion with colleagues

For the newly appointed subject coordinator, monitoring and evaluation through one of the forms listed above is a good starting point, although the skills and knowledge needed for all such activities cannot be overstated. The processes must be carried out rigorously if they are going to be purposeful, and so it can be appreciated that the coordinator needs to have the subject expertise necessary for carrying out the activities, and for making recommendations based on the judgments made. Even though the activities listed above are good starting points for the coordinator, it is essential that advice is sought from more experienced colleagues before, during and after carrying out any of them; to aid the coordinator in planning and carrying out the activity, in using the results of the activity to make judgements and recommendations for future action, and then in evaluating and reflecting upon his or her own performance. This is necessary for the coordinator to become proficient in this aspect of coordination and to prepare the coordinator for the important processes of monitoring and evaluation of lessons.

For monitoring and evaluation activities to be purposeful tools in developing the subject, a framework for each activity must be identified, which will set out the rationale for the activity and record the outcomes. The school may use a standard framework, or the coordinator may need to devise one of their own. Again, there are many sources of support for the coordinator in devising his or her own format for the framework, both those sources noted in earlier sections of the book, and also sample frameworks readily available for use. The checklist below sets out the information to be recorded during these monitoring and evaluation activities and thus sections to be included in the monitoring and evaluation activity format:

✓ Date of monitoring and evaluation activity

✓ Focus of activity – e.g. attainment of children, appropriateness of planned activity

✓ Context of activity – e.g. monitoring planning, assessing outcomes

✓ Other staff involved

✓ Criteria for judgments

✓ Judgments made in response to activity

✓ Evidence for judgments

✓ Comments made by other staff involved

✓ Recommendations made following monitoring and evaluation

It is important that other members of staff are involved in all monitoring and evaluation activities, as it is the staff that will act on the results of the processes. By recording the comments of other staff involved, the coordinator is recognizing the significant part they play in the activity, and thus the significant part they play in improving the planning and delivery of the subject in school.

When the coordinator is ready to carry out a lesson observation as a monitoring and evaluation activity, it is imperative that he or she again seeks the support of more experienced colleagues. This support may be in the form of advice or guidance, or the inexperienced subject coordinator may observe a lesson by a more experienced but sympathetic teacher who will, in turn, provide the coordinator with feedback regarding the coordinator's performance. A shared observation may be an appropriate approach, as this allows for a comparison of observations and judgments made. A further approach may be to conduct an observation of a videoed lesson. All these approaches will aid the coordinator in developing the skills and confidence necessary for this important task. Again, a framework for the monitoring and evaluation of the lesson must be used; a lesson observation is a formal process and so the activity is to be recorded accordingly. There are many formats for lesson observation forms, and each school will probably have its own format for use by the subject coordinator: what is important is that the information to be recorded is done so accurately, professionally and in a way that fully reflects the nature of the lesson observed. The checklist below presents an extensive list of the information to be recorded during a lesson observation, together with recommendations for judgments that may be made:

✓ Factual information regarding the class, year group, teacher in charge of the lesson, timing of the lesson

✓ Introduction to the lesson – does the teacher inform the children of the objective of the lesson (what they will learn) and establish high expectations?

✓ Are objectives appropriate to the national curriculum requirements of the subject and appropriate to the year group being taught?

✓ Does the objective relate to previous work carried out by the children?

✓ Body of the lesson – is it well-structured with a suitable pace?

✓ Subject knowledge – does the teacher use his or her subject knowledge appropriately within the lesson?

✓ Teaching method – what is the use of whole class, group and individual teaching? Is there a high proportion of direct teaching?

✓ Resources – are resources used appropriately? Are they well-made, good quality resources which are appropriate for the task?

✓ Differentiation – are all needs catered for through effective differentiation?

✓ Questioning – is good use of questioning made throughout the lesson?

✓ Involvement of children – are all children adequately involved?

Successful Subject Co-ordination

✓ Language – is appropriate language used through-out? Is subject-specific language developed and used?

✓ Opportunities – are there opportunities for children to demonstrate, explain, discuss and practice their ideas? Are they encouraged to watch, listen, and be involved in practical work and solving problems?

✓ Support staff – are support staff used well to support the teaching and learning?

✓ Plenary – is there a purposeful end to the lesson where key aspects are reinforced and misconceptions dealt with? Are indications to the next objective to be covered by the children given?

✓ Homework – is relevant homework set for the children to continue to engage in the subject matter?

✓ Children's attitudes – what were the children's attitudes to learning during the lesson? Did they respond with enthusiasm, listen attentively, speak appropriately, participate confidently, concentrate well, persevere, work independently without direct supervision, work well alone or with a partner or in a group, select and use resources sensibly? Did the children evaluate and modify their work?

✓ Behaviour – was the behaviour of the children what is to be expected?

✓ Relationships – does the teacher achieve good relationships with the children?

✓ Attainment – was the children's attainment in the lesson appropriate? Was it above, the same as or below the expectations for the age group? What was the attainment of particular groups of children – those with special educational needs, English as an additional language, gifted children?

(www.cleo.net.uk 2003)

Following a lesson observation, feedback must be given to the teacher who was observed, as a matter of courtesy initially but also to support their professional development in teaching. Formal monitoring and evaluation of teaching is carried out in schools as part of the Performance Management Policy and the subject coordinator may be involved in lesson observations that feed in to this process, in addition to developing the subject provision in school. It is therefore most important that this part of the monitoring and evaluation activity – the feedback to the observed – is dealt with honestly and sympathetically. The coordinator will comment on all aspects of the lesson observed and be able to discuss the weaknesses of the lesson as well as the strengths.

The requirement for subject coordinators to carry out monitoring and evaluation activities gives teachers within a school the collective responsibility to ensure the processes are carried out and used to develop both the planning and delivery of the curriculum as a whole. Each teacher who is a subject coordinator will carry out monitoring and evaluation activities within their own subject and so the processes have become two-way, with each teacher leading monitoring and evaluation and, in other subjects, being led through monitoring and evaluation activities. The modern subject coordinator therefore now has a real responsibility in developing teaching and learning across the school in all subjects, not solely in the subject they are leading.

7

Ofsted

Ofsted Inspections are carried out in maintained schools at least once every six years, although the time between inspections varies from school to school. An Ofsted team will spend time in a school observing lessons, meeting staff – including the subject coordinators – and reading school documentation. The inspection team also consults parents, governors and children. The inspection, and the subsequent report, will focus on the quality of education provided, the educational standards achieved, the leadership and management of the school, the management of finances and the spiritual, moral, social and cultural development of the pupils. It is accepted that the role of the subject coordinator is a management role, and so the subject will be inspected with respect to teaching and learning, the attainment of children and the leadership and management of the school. It is important at the time of inspection that the subject coordinator, even the newly appointed co-ordinator, has an overview of the subject in school and a vision for where the subject provision is going. Ofsted inspections are intended to aid a school's improvement through identifying strengths to be built on and weaknesses to be addressed; the effective subject coordinator will already have a notion of what the subject's strengths and weaknesses are, and this will aid in writing the Ofsted Action Plan.

Successful Subject Co-ordination

Following the Ofsted visit, an inspection report is issued to the school. This summarizes the findings of the Ofsted team and, for each subject area, includes comments relating to teaching, learning, children's attainment and the management of the subject. The subject coordinator will then be expected to work with the headteacher, the senior management team and the governors to formulate a plan of action that builds on the noted successes and addresses the identified weaknesses of all aspects of the subject. This requires the coordinator to be able to interpret the inspection comments made, accept them as a true reflection of the school's provision for the subject and put together a course of action in response to the changes indicated. The report may point to a range of personal and professional changes to be made: the checklist below sets out some of the main changes that may be required:

✓ A change to established routines and practices

✓ A change to documentation for the subject

✓ A possible redundancy of old resources and the need for new resources

✓ The revision, renewal or learning of subject-specific knowledge and skills

✓ Training for individual teachers, a group of teachers or the whole staff

✓ The revision, renewal or learning of subject-specific assessment techniques

✓ A revision of previously held beliefs and ideas

The subject coordinator can thus expect to be fully involved in the inspection process and its follow-up, in consultation with the headteacher, governors and senior management team. It can be appreciated that the Ofsted process of preparing for inspection, the inspection itself, the receiving of the inspection report, the resulting action plan and work carried out as part of the action plan is one of the main vehicles for demonstrating the skills of the successful subject coordinator. The coordinator must have the expertise to prepare the documentation needed for the inspection, to support staff through the inspection and to respond to the findings. He or she must firstly have the skills to read the Ofsted inspection report and, more importantly, be able to interpret what has been stated. Indeed, the ability to read and interpret subject-specific documentation is not only a requirement during the Ofsted process, but is needed during the course of day-to-day coordination of the subject. The school curriculum has been in a constant period of change for some years with numerous initiatives, strategies and curriculum updates: all require a response from schools at a local level and it is usual that the coordinator is involved in preparing this. The inspection report may make statements that the coordinator, and the school, may not initially agree with. However, it is part of the coordinator's role to accept the findings as a true reflection of the school's provision for the subject, and to provide a framework for developing the subject accordingly. It may be helpful to remember that the Ofsted report details what has been observed during a short space of time and what is apparent through documentation provided by the school. The report therefore acknowledges what is discernable to an external observer and it is this that is to be improved upon.

The coordinator must be mindful here of the reaction of the staff to the inspection report, particularly of staff whose own teaching may have been found less than satisfactory. The staff may experience loss of confidence and self-esteem and so the coordinator must be able to interpret the report and put together an action plan that will address the inspection issues yet motivate the staff to develop their practice. This obviously requires great sensitivity and empathy from the coordinator. In order to aid the staff in accessing the findings of the report in a meaningful way, the coordinator may re-present the findings in summary form, identifying the key points of the report that need action. Again, this demonstrates the skills the coordinator must have, in order to summarize the report, identify the changes needed, and then to work out a plan of action and to effect the change.

The points for action may relate to a change in policy, a change in practice or a change in coordination. They may require change by one member of staff, a group or the whole staff. They may be of relevance to one key stage, or to more than one key stage. The coordinator therefore not only identifies the points for action, but also categorizes them according to who is to be involved in the change. This demonstrates the need for good organizational skills.

The points for action then feed into the official response to the inspection report compiled by the headteacher, senior management team and the governors. (Presently the school has at least one week from receipt of the draft report to comment on matters of factual accuracy, and 40 school working days from the receipt of the full report to respond in writing.) It is then the responsibility of the governors to prepare a Governors' Statement and the responsibility of the subject coordinator to prepare a written action plan, to be submitted to the Ofsted team. The action plan will follow the same format as the coordinator's action plan discussed in Chapter 2. Similarly, it will include details of the authors of the plan and those responsible for its implementation, specific target and action to be taken, criteria for success and review dates. Crucially, it will also include details of the members of staff who will be involved in the action.

Once the action plan has been written, it must be approved by the school's governing body and subsequently by the Ofsted inspection team, and then presented to the staff. This begins the process of developing teaching and learning across the school, through initiating and leading staff development. The action to be taken may involve the use of many of the approaches noted throughout the book, from support- ing individual staff in their subject-specific develop- ment to a series of staff meetings and/or In-service days, from informal workshops to demonstration lessons. Whatever means is identified by the coordinator, it must be remembered that the purpose of the action plan is to ensure all staff have sufficient knowledge and understanding to deliver quality teaching and learning that leads to improved attain- ment by the children. It can thus be appreciated how the Ofsted process requires the subject coordinator to use the many skills identified throughout this book.

As noted, when introducing the summary of the inspection report and the action plan to the staff the coordinator must act with sensitivity. Depending upon the extent of the change proposed in the action plan, the staff may either be supportive of the action or oppose the action. Change may be required that is minor or, much more rarely, major in effect; it may be needed with respect to staff knowledge and under-standing, or to curriculum practice. However, not all the members of staff may be willing or able to accept such change, and so the coordinator must be able to clearly identify the changes to be made, understand the implications of the proposed changes, set a programme for change and deliver the programme. A good starting point for the coordinator is to use the introduction to the action plan required by Ofsted. The introduction sets out the aims of the action plan and the means by which they will be achieved, and is thus an excellent means of summarizing the action to be taken, for both the inspection response and the staff. A sample statement is presented below:

The principal aim of the subject action plan is to raise the attainment of the children in . . . . It builds on the positive aspects of the Inspection report and focuses on staff training, monitoring the delivery of the subject and general support to be given by the subject coordinator. Staff training will take place over one term, through weekly staff meetings and an INSET day. The scheme of work will be reviewed and monitoring of teaching and learning will be based on the scheme of work. The coordinator will continue to keep up to date with current ideas in the teaching of the subject and use this to support colleagues.

The changes to be made may relate to one aspect or to numerous aspects of the subject, to one member of staff or to numerous members of staff. However, all staff need to be aware of the findings of the report and relate them to their own teaching. Again this requires great sensitivity – indeed, many, if not all, the knowledge, skills, understandings and attributes of the subject coordinator will be much in evidence during this time. The coordinator must be able to recognize, accept and work with the range of feelings that change may inspire in some of the staff. These feelings may be intensified if there are changes to be made to their individual practice in a number of areas within the subject, or across a range of subjects in the curriculum. Indeed, the subject coordinator must support their colleagues through this stage, and meanwhile may have to deal with their own feelings with regard to the change needed. However, the more up to date the coordinator is on issues regarding the teaching and learning of the subject, the more confident he or she will feel about the change and the more able in supporting and motivating the staff. The subject coordinator must be mindful at this time that they are the subject *expert* and so their reaction to change may be very different to that of the other, non-specialist, staff. It may be helpful here for the subject coordinator to reflect on their own feelings when changes have been introduced in other subjects, and use this to support their colleagues.

The reactions of the staff cannot always be anticipated, as everyone can find him- or herself supporting or opposing change at different times.

Successful Subject Co-ordination

Reactions to change may be dependant on a number of factors: the immediate circumstances, the nature of the change proposed and individual personalities. It is important for the subject coordinator to be aware of the possible responses, as this will help in planning for the implementation of change. The change may be perceived as an exciting opportunity that offers teachers an opening to experiment with their teaching and to be creative in their interpretation of the curriculum. Alternatively, it may be perceived as threatening to the teacher's interpretation of the curriculum and critical of their present practice. There are many factors that may influence the response to change to practice, including:

- The origin of the change: for example, those that originate nationally, and are thus backed by the force of national legislation, have potentially considerably more impetus than locally originated change

- The amount of input the teachers may have on the change

- Changes that are internally inspired, albeit possibly more relevant to the development needs of the nursery/school, may be viewed as less effective than national developments

- Everyday pressures on teachers – planning, paperwork, assessment, etc.

- External pressures on teachers and on teacher time

- Priority in the curriculum for literacy, numeracy and ICT skills

- The perceived threat of the change to the stability of the curriculum

- Anxiety about the new skills and knowledge needed

- Concerns based on a professional assessment of the proposals

- Concerns, worries and consequent resistance based on emotional responses

- An already recognized need to implement change

- A forum for developing creativity

A further consideration at this time is that there may be many subject coordinators in the school trying to develop their subject in response to the inspection report. The effects of this on the staff may be positive or negative: it may motivate the staff or demotivate them. What is needed is a coordinated approach to the implementation of the Ofsted action plans; indeed, this is the responsibility of the head-teacher. Such a response may result in staff meetings shared between subject coordinators, where the skills to be developed are cross-curricular. The subject coordinator will therefore demonstrate his or her ability to work within a team, whilst promoting development within the subject they lead. There is a danger that if the individual coordinators do not work together there will be an information overload for the staff, resulting in the action taken being ineffective. A coordinated approach ensures that all subjects are represented, either in shared activities or within an organized series of staff meetings. This also demonstrates the contribution that the subject coordinator can make to the curriculum as a whole. He or she must be able to present a well-reasoned and clear rationale for the subject provision in school, explaining how it is to be developed, and to state clearly and succinctly how the subject can contribute to the complete learning process and thus the wider curriculum. The rationale must be responsive to the teaching and learning in the subject, and thus to the needs of the children in the class situation, in order that each child's potential may be fully developed. The subject coordinator will thereby establish the crucial role the subject plays in the National Curriculum and the school's curriculum by offering the possibility of integrated development across the physical, social, creative, cognitive and aesthetic dimensions and establish the complementary nature of the subject with other subjects.

One of the most difficult areas the subject coordinator will work within as a result of an inspection is supporting the weak teacher in developing his or her teaching. An immense amount of patience and sensitivity is needed here and it is most important that the teacher being supported accepts that the subject coordinator is there in a supportive rather than a judgemental role. The process must begin with the coordinator aiding the teacher in identifying his or her own successes in the subject, and then a personal action plan that builds on these needs to be set in place. Although this is a difficult time for both the subject coordinator and the teacher being supported, it also brings great rewards. The most important skill to use here is empathy, so that the coordinator can understand the process the supported teacher is going through. The development of a good working relationship is also essential to the success of the support being put into place. The range of skills to be exhibited here by the coordinator can be clearly discerned. Again, time and organization are major features of the development programme – the need to set goals for the supported teacher and a time scale for their achievement will help the coordinator in targeting support appropriately and aid the supported teacher in visualizing the progress being made.

An Ofsted inspection, and the resulting work by the subject coordinator, thus necessitates the use of a range of skills and attributes. In addition to those already noted, the effective subject coordinator will also:

- Establish credibility with the headteacher, senior management team, staff and governors

- Develop his or her own ability to work with and alongside other subject coordinators

- Know how to involve others in developments in the teaching and learning of the subject being led

- Be direct in recognizing and praising the achievements of others

- Set attainable and realistic targets for staff and children

8

Developing the Role

It has been demonstrated throughout this book how the effective subject coordinator will be involved in numerous tasks, all leading towards the development of the subject being led and, accordingly, advances in teaching, learning and achievement of the children. The number of areas for the coordinator to consider when developing the role is also vast! Accordingly, a definitive list of activities within the wider role of the subject coordinator cannot be offered to the newly appointed coordinator – however, the range of tasks may now be categorized:

- Personal development

- Providing a model of good practice for other staff

- Support and guidance for individual teachers and groups of teachers

- Leading planning and assessment in the subject

- Planning and delivering subject-specific In-service

- Monitoring and evaluating the provision of the subject

- Arranging and leading meetings

- Providing school documentation

Successful Subject Co-ordination

- Resource management
- Working with other adults
- Representing the school beyond the school day

This chapter considers some of the many tasks involved in these broad areas, although some have been covered in detail in earlier sections of the book. Personal development of the coordinator has been considered throughout: indeed, this book has taken the reader on a journey from the first tentative steps a newly appointed coordinator will be expected to take, to the wider implications of the role and how it may be carried out in school. It must be remembered, however, that personal development is on-going: as the requirements of the subject being led change over time, so must the knowledge, skills and understandings of the coordinator. The successful subject coordinator will continue therefore to update his or her knowledge of teaching and learning within the subject and across the curriculum, knowledge of how to work with staff and the skills needed to effect the relevant action being put into place, and knowledge and skills needed to lead development in the subject.

The requirement that the coordinator provide a model of good practice for other staff has not yet been explored within the book, although it was acknowledged that the coordinator could motivate others by displaying personal enthusiasm and motivation. Being a good role model suggests that the coordinator develops good practice in the subject and displays this through all the activities he or she is involved in. An excellent example of this is presenting model lessons. Through these the subject coordinator is able to lead the professional development of staff by example, to demonstrate to staff how to put policy into practice and to display enthusiasm for the subject. Although this requires confidence on the part of the subject coordinator, and may be best left until the coordinator feels that he or she has the level of expertise to share with others, it is an excellent way of supporting staff in their needs and does ensure reflective practice by the coordinator. The benefits of successful model lessons are manifold. The coordinator will use the model lessons to demonstrate the requirements of a successful lesson (as noted in Chapter 6), and will also, hopefully, inspire and motivate staff to develop their teaching of the subject and to promote innovation in the subject. The model lesson may also aid in the promoting of teamwork and mutual support between the staff. By carrying out the model lesson the coordinator is inviting comment on both the teaching and on subject-specific matters. The lesson thus opens up dialogue and may provide a means of communication between the coordinator and the more reluctant member of staff. In turn, it offers a means of evaluating practice and promotes accountability.

Support and guidance for individual teachers and groups of teachers may be actioned in so many ways, from informal impromptu requests for ideas to more formal, planned activities. Obviously the impromptu requests cannot be pre-empted and so the coordinator has to respond accordingly to each request. If support and guidance cannot be given at the time of asking the coordinator must respond at an appropriate time, to be agreed with the teacher requesting the information or assistance. The coordinator may be able to support individuals or groups of colleagues through the provision of workshops. Workshops are a fairly informal means of working with colleagues as they allow for sharing experiences between the staff. Planning and delivering workshops provides a level of support that lies between the very formal require-ments of INSET and the informal day-to-day requests for support. Through workshops, relevant and focused assistance can be offered and, in turn, the newly appointed coordinator may use the workshops to develop their own training skills, before working with the whole staff in more formal INSET situations.

Another group of teachers or individuals that may require direct support by the subject coordinator comprises trainee and newly qualified teachers. The support to be offered here may be very specific to the trainee or newly qualified teacher's needs. In order to fulfill these specific needs, the subject coordinator must develop a working knowledge of the require-ments for the award of Qualified Teacher Status – indeed, these standards are an excellent introduction to the needs of the subject and so form a helpful resource for the newly appointed subject coordinator. An awareness of the Career Entry Profile and standards for induction is also needed when support-ing trainee teachers and newly qualified teachers.

The need to lead planning and assessment in the subject has been briefly considered earlier in this book. Leading planning and assessment enables the subject coordinator to directly influence the teaching of the subject in school, in assessing the outcomes and in monitoring the attainment of the children. The coordinator may be called upon to lead curriculum medium- and/or short-term planning and to aid groups of teachers and/or individuals, in response to an audit following an Ofsted inspection (as discussed in Chapter 7). Alternatively, curriculum planning, organization and delivery may form part of the coordinator's on-going role within the school. The subject coordinator will use the overview of the curriculum in school that they have developed to support individual planning needs and will thus be able to provide concrete assistance in planning by providing ideas and establishing how quality teaching and learning in the subject may be achieved. For the curriculum leader to be most effective in leading and directing a whole school approach to planning for the subject, there must be open-minded cooperation between the staff and agreement of a common approach to teaching and learning. This goes beyond the notion of the curriculum leader designing and delivering a total package and thus requires the teacher (or teachers) being supported to enter into a partnership with the coordinator to devise a relevant, coherent plan for teaching and learning. The curriculum leader therefore offers the class teacher support in deciding the content of lessons, planning their delivery, resourcing lessons, evaluating lessons and assessing the outcomes of lessons, while the teacher offers the coordinator support in deciding the appropriateness of the suggestions made to the children to be taught.

Assessment issues within a subject is yet another huge area to consider but, nevertheless, it is one of the features of successful subject coordination that the coordinator is fully involved in the assessment, record keeping and reporting of pupils' progress within the subject. Obviously, the assessment coordinator in school will provide guidance on this aspect of the role: what is important is that the subject coordinator has an overview of assessment, record keeping and reporting of pupils' progress within the subject and is directly responsible for planning and organizing agreement trials of assessed work. The coordinator must therefore possess the knowledge needed to accurately assess children's work against national standards. As a result of these agreement trials (also known as assessment conferences) the coordinator will begin a portfolio of assessed work. This is an essential document for both the coordinator and the school, as it is used as a benchmark for individual teachers when assessing children's work in the subject. It also provides evidence for the coordinator when making judgements about whether the children in school are making acceptable progress in the subject, and will thus aid the coordinator in setting future targets for the subject. The use of local and national data to support the setting of targets is also to be noted. The data can be used to identify under, and over, achievement in the subject and suggest methods or action to support the children. The coordinator must therefore be able to analyse and interpret relevant national and local school data, alongside research and inspection evidence, to inform policies, practices, expectations, targets and teaching methods. The coordinator is then able to use all this information to identify realistic and challenging targets for improvement in the subject.

It is accepted that a feature of subject coordination is the planning and delivery of In-service training (INSET) in the school-based setting; indeed, this is one of the main vehicles for communicating with the staff as a whole. The aim for INSET is always the same – to empower and enskill the teaching staff: this may be achieved through increasing teachers' knowledge and skills, reinforcing current thinking, or promoting innovation. INSET may be required following an Ofsted inspection (see Chapter 7), after a curricular audit, following policy change or after a change in staff. In planning INSET the coordinator should use the findings of both the audit for the subject and his or her monitoring and evaluation activities to highlight the areas for development. INSET may thus form part of the subject coordinator's action plan, the Ofsted response or the School Improvement Plan. Again, the newly appointed subject coordinator will need to seek advice and guidance on planning and delivering school-specific INSET. This can be sought from the headteacher and/or experienced colleagues, and may require consultation with the Local Education Authority advisor for the subject.

In addition to leading whole staff training, the subject coordinator may also be required to coordinate a package of high-quality continued professional development for individual members of staff. Sources of support for this include institutions of higher education, the Local Education Authority and the professional body for the subject. All In-service provision must be discussed with the headteacher.

Monitoring and evaluating the provision of the subject being led has been covered extensively (see Chapter 6). However, the provision of school-based and externally provided professional development in the subject both utilize the information gained through monitoring and evaluation and feed back into the monitoring and evaluation of the subject provision. This demonstrates clearly how each facet of the role supports the coordination of the subject as a whole.

The development of communication skills has been covered above (Chapter 5). These skills are necessary for all interactions with staff, a further requirement of which is to arrange and lead meetings. The term 'meetings' can be used to cover a range of situations, from one-to-one interactions to discussions involving the whole staff. Such interactions have already been considered, under a variety of headings: the coordinator will also be involved in leading a number of subject-specific meetings, for example, meetings with the headteacher, senior management team and governors to keep them informed about subject policies, plans, priorities and achievements; staff meetings and parents' evenings. Liaison meetings are needed between staff and between subject areas to ensure all children's needs are met with respect to the subject. It is the skill of the coordinator that ensures that a meeting is deemed a success by all involved. Successful meetings must:

- Be necessary! It must be considered to be the most efficient method of communication

- Be held in an appropriate setting or venue

- Have a clear purpose, which is shared with the attendees

- Be of relevance to the attendees

- Have an agenda that is used, given out to participants before the meeting starts, and is adhered to

- Balance the needs of the task in hand, the individual attendees and the group of attendees as a whole

- Involve colleagues as active participants in the meeting, rather than passive recipients

- Ensure that the group is able to function as a team in which individuals feel valued

- Provide participants with copies of all documentation needed or under discussion

- Ensure all information is communicated accurately

- Allow for an exchange of ideas

- Generate a general agreement and consensus of opinion

- Result in a commitment to a particular course of action or decision

- Inspire the attendees

- Result in the attendees being enthusiastic about the recommendations of the meeting

- Lead to success for all concerned

◆ Result in the meeting being considered a good use of the attendees' time

◆ Be chaired effectively (see below)

◆ Have minutes taken, to ensure that an accurate record of the meeting is kept

◆ Have an outcome which can be evaluated

Organizing and chairing a meeting consequently needs careful preparation, from considering whether a meeting is the most effective method of communication to whether the meeting will involve dialogue only or will require more active participation by the members. It may be helpful for the coordinator to think back to both a successful meeting he or she has attended and one which was less successful, in order to consider what made it successful/unsuccessful and how a meeting can be structured to both suit the style of delivery of the coordinator and result in the meeting being deemed a success. The checklist below provides the coordinator with advice on how to chair a meeting effectively:

✓ Use the agenda well, to structure the meeting, keep it on track and on time

✓ Listen to everyone

✓ Seek clarification of comments made

✓ Encourage all participants to be involved

✓ Summarize the discussion points at various intervals

✓ Keep the discussion to the point and moving at a good pace

✓ Use non-verbal gestures and/or statements to draw people back to the original agenda

✓ Referee the discussion – argument and disagreement is productive within a meeting, but must not be allowed to descend to aggression or bullying

An essential requirement in developing the co-ordination role is to provide school documentation and correspondence. It will not be a surprise to know that there are numerous demands on the coordinator relating to this responsibility! It is through documentation and correspondence that the school's commitment to the subject is demonstrated and so all paperwork produced must be relevant to the information being conveyed, appropriate to school needs and reflect both local and national guidelines regarding the subject. School documentation and correspondence may take the form of letters, handbooks for parents, handbooks for staff, staff newsletters, policy statements, and schemes of work, and thus may be targeted at parents, governors, staff, the local community or the Local Education Authority. The documentation may be formal, as in the subject policy, or informal, as in messages and newsletters to staff – indeed, newsletters are essential tools for the effective subject coordinator. They may be used to convey up-to-date information to parents, governors and staff without the need for a formal meeting. Newsletters for staff are particularly helpful when subject coordinators need to update their colleagues on current thinking within the subject and provide new ideas for activities and new resources in school but staff meeting time is unavailable. It must, however, be remembered that it is through school documentation that the school's interpretation of national guidelines on the curriculum is conveyed to others and so it is vitally important that it is adhered to, for it lays the foundations for good practice in subject teaching. The documentation produced must therefore be appropriate, good quality and well-presented. The coordinator may be responsible for writing a part of the documentation (for example, a statement regarding the description and outline of the teaching of each subject in school) or may be responsible for writing the whole document (for example, a staff subject-specific newsletter). The checklist below provides guidance for the subject coordinator in planning and/or contributing to a range of school documentation:

✓ Is the document needed at this time, and an appropriate vehicle to use?

✓ Is the documentation new or does it involve revising past documentation?

✓ Is there a school model to follow?

✓ Access the Local Education Authority model and other models available

✓ Use the models to provide headings/areas for inclusion in school documentation

✓ Consider the audience for the documentation

✓ Consider the use of language for the documentation – informal or formal, worded for the professional or non-professional

✓ Is it appropriate to include a selection of children's work in the subject area, to enhance the comments made in writing and provide evidence of the policy in practice?

✓ Use carefully the drafting process – produce a first draft, circulate to colleagues and invite colleagues to comment on draft, add ideas, etc.

✓ If necessary, delegate small groups to discuss and review the draft documentation

✓ Use feedback given by colleagues to redraft final version of documentation

✓ Present the final draft to the headteacher and, if appropriate, to the school governors for approval

At some time in their coordination of a subject area the subject coordinator will review current policy and prepare an updated document. A subject policy is a very important document that sets out succinctly the school's overall rationale for the teaching of the subject. Policies are used as reference documents for staff and governors and must be relevant to the whole school. The policy should be written in plain English and be concise yet comprehensive. Another tall order! The format of such policies is at the discretion of the school and so a reviewed policy will follow the school's guidelines: however, a standard subject policy will need to contain the following information:

◆ Date of policy

◆ Author of policy

◆ Date policy was approved by full Governing Body

Successful Subject Co-ordination

- Date of next review
- School's philosophy regarding the subject
- Rationale for the inclusion of the subject in the curriculum
- Aims – what skills, knowledge and understanding will be developed
- Organization of the subject – how teaching and learning will be planned and delivered, making reference to the national documentation for the subject
- Use of ICT in the subject
- Assessment, record keeping and reporting
- Special needs provision
- Equal opportunities and multicultural issues
- Health and safety issues
- Reference to other policies – particularly literacy, numeracy and ICT skills, and other cross-curricular links
- Links with the wider community – visits out of school, visitors into school, etc.
- Resources
- The role of the coordinator
- The role of the headteacher
- The role of the governors

(www.cleo.net.uk 2003)

Linked directly to the school policy for a specific subject is the Scheme of Work. Schemes of Work give details of how the policy is put into practice, by detailing how the requirements of national documentation are to be taught in the school, thus setting out the planning and organization of the subject through school. The school may use a commercial Scheme of Work for the subject, the relevant QCA exemplar Scheme of Work or may have its own devised by the subject coordinator and the staff. It is important that the Scheme of Work is relevant to the needs of the school and is used to establish good standards of work in all year groups as well as continuity and progression across, and between, key stages. It is therefore important that the subject coordinator has a clear vision about moving children's learning on in the school so that they grow in knowledge and deepen their understanding of the subject. With this in mind, the subject coordinator may need to amend a commercial Scheme of Work or the QCA exemplar Scheme of Work to ensure that the objectives to be delivered in each year group are relevant and set out alongside suitable ideas for activities. Such activities will therefore be age-appropriate, used to reinforce key skills regularly and will motivate children into serious and deep thinking about the subject. A comprehensive Scheme of Work thus includes:

◆ A rationale – how the scheme came to be written

◆ Units of work – statements relating to the subject being delivered in linked topics, individual units or on-going work

Successful Subject Co-ordination

- Overview of coverage – how national requirements are allocated to year groups

- Termly topics – overview of suggested cross-
  curricular topics

- Yearly coverage – detailed coverage of national
  requirements

- Assessment – details of formative, summative and
  statutory assessments

- End-of-year expectations in the subject – matching
  children's outcomes to the National Curriculum
  level descriptions.

In order to put the subject policy into practice,
through the Scheme of Work, the activities listed
must be resourced accordingly. Many schools now
involve subject coordinators directly in resource
management – the purchasing and organizing of
subject-specific resources. The successful subject
coordinator will therefore ensure that the subject
being led is adequately resourced with well-made,
good quality and appropriate resources that are
matched to the children's needs and the outcomes
required. One of the first tasks of the newly appointed
coordinator is to audit the current resources and then
to advise on, and coordinate, the acquisition of new
materials. There must be an on-going commitment to
ensure old, out-dated resources are discarded and
new, subject-specific resources are purchased on a
regular basis, and so the coordinator must be mindful
of the need to consider value for money. The subject
coordinator is responsible for ensuring the resources

are organized well and used efficiently, effectively and safely, and so a storage system must be used that ensures existing resources are maintained and accessible, while allowing for new resources from a wide range of sources inside and outside the school to be incorporated into the system.

Throughout this book the need for the subject coordinator to work with other teachers has been considered in detail, and the need to communicate with the governors, parents, the local community and the Local Education Authority has also been noted. It is through these interactions that the school's accountability for the ethos, interpretation and delivery of the subject is assured. The notion of accountability for the curriculum is not new; indeed, it has been developing since the late 1970s, although it was the Education Acts of 1980, 1981, 1986 and 1988 that made schools truly publicly accountable (Docking 1990). There was an increasing emphasis on parental rights within the Education Acts from 1980 to 1993 and so schools are required to develop good relationships between parents and schools, with this being considered to be an essential requisite for providing the optimum education for children. Keeping parents informed of the curriculum is therefore no longer a courtesy: informed parents are better able to support their children and the school. The effective subject coordinator must therefore support the school in its accountability for the subject being led, and so must be able to communicate effectively with all partners in the education process. This will involve the coordinator informing these different partners of the school's interpretation and delivery of the subject area and the children's attainment; there are many ways in which the subject coordinator is able to achieve this, including meetings, school correspondence and themed curriculum events.

Themed curriculum events are an excellent vehicle for enhancing others' perceptions of how a subject is taught and what children learn and so parents, governors, Local Education Authority representatives and representatives from the community may be invited to attend. The events may be held during the school day, for example, a themed day or week when all work carried out by the children is related to the subject area, or immediately after school (or even later in the evening), for example, curriculum evenings when the delivery of the subject may be demonstrated and the adults attending may be involved in a 'lesson'.

Other valuable workforces within the school are classroom assistants and volunteers. These adults assist the class teacher in providing differentiated work across the curriculum, work that is matched to individual needs and abilities. The subject coordinator therefore must also work with these adults, to develop and maintain both their knowledge and understanding of the subject and an enthusiasm for it. All of the advice offered to the coordinator thus far is applicable for working with these adults, although it must be remembered that they are non-specialists and not trained teachers, and so support from the coordinator must be matched to their individual needs. Workshops, as discussed earlier, are a particularly effective means of working with classroom assistants and volunteers.

One final consideration within this section of the book is that of the subject coordinator representing the school beyond the school day. Attendance at subject-specific meetings and consultations with outside agencies has already been noted: an important area for the effective subject coordinator's attention is that of cross-phase liaison. When children move through the key stages – from the Foundation Stage to Key Stage 1, from Key Stage 1 to Key Stage 2 and from Key Stage 2 to Key Stage 3 – the requirements of the curriculum inevitably change but do build on previous teaching and learning, and so an understanding by teachers is needed of what children have experienced in the subject in previous years. 'Liaison' is the term used to describe how teachers from each key stage receive information about the children. The subject coordinator therefore has a particular role to play in managing liaison between key stages.

Liaison may involve meetings, joint projects and/or the transfer of written information. Copies of children's Records of Achievement now form part of a child's educational record and schools are required to transfer this information when a child transfers to a new school. A common transfer form is now used to send information about the child, including key stage test results and teacher assessments, to the receiving school and/or key stage. The coordinator may be involved in the completion of transfer forms or may oversee completion. However, this is the minimum liaison that may take place and yet there is much more that schools can do to both aid the transition for the children and provide information for the receiving

93

key stage. The checklist below lists some liaison activities that the coordinator may organize:

✓ Meetings between teachers – to build up professional relationships

✓ Agree common objectives for the meetings

✓ Set a programme of meeting dates – to keep the process going

✓ Set agenda – to ensure meetings are used for the purpose of liaison issues

✓ Chair meetings – to keep involved in the liaison process

✓ Encourage equal contribution to the meetings – all teachers involved need to be able to contribute to the planning and delivery of liaison

✓ Team teaching – teachers sharing teaching

✓ Cross-phase teaching – teachers moving between key stages

✓ Shared planning – to ensure team teaching and/ or cross-phase teaching is relevant to the children being taught

✓ Exchange of examples of children's work – to increase awareness of children's achievements

✓ Cross-phase assessment moderation – to develop a common understanding of national standards

✓ Cross-phase assessments – an assessment activity carried out in each year group, the results of which can be discussed and moderated

✓ Joint curriculum projects – a projec when the children are in one phase and completed in the subseque education

✓ Cross-phase medium-term plann continuity and progression in the s

This brief look at the development coordinator's role has demonstrated extent of the role, and the depth of kr and understandings needed by the c how far the individual coordinator ma Successful coordination is about deve and learning and the attainment of subject, and the means to achieve th are manifold. The effective subject c therefore determine for his or herself v will be used to effect good subject school, and then systematically worl menting them. The only boundary to time. This has been noted repeatedl book but only now, when the full e has been outlined, is the coordina grasp what can be done and th against what can be achieved in tl This balance is the key to su coordination.

(Cheshire Coun

References and Further Reading

Alexander, R., Rose, J. & Woodhead, C. (1992) *Curriculum Organisation and Classroom Practice in Primary Schools: A Discussion Paper*. DES: London.

Bentley, D. and Watts, M. (1994) *Teaching and Learning in Primary Science and Technology*. Open University Press: Buckingham.

Busher, H., Harris, A. and Wise, C. (2000) *Subject Leadership and School Improvement*. Paul Chapman: London.

Cheshire County Council (1997) *Bubbles: Bridging the Gap KS2/3 Liaison*. Zeneca: Cheshire.

Docking, J. (1990) *Primary Schools and Parents: Rights, Responsibilities and Relationships*. Hodder and Stoughton: London.

Fleming, P. and Amesbury, M. (2001) *The Art of Middle Management in Primary Schools: A Guide to Effective Subject, Year and Team Leadership.* David Fulton: London.

Harrison, S. and Theaker, K. (1989) *Curriculum Leadership and Co-ordination in the Primary School: A Handbook for Teachers*. Guild House Press: Whalley.

Hornby, G. (2000) *Improving Parental Involvement*. Cassell: London and New York.

Jenkin, M., Jones, Jeff & Lord, S. (2000) *Monitoring and Evaluation for School Improvement*. Heinemann: Oxford.

Middlewood, D. and Burton, N. (2001) (eds) *Managing the Curriculum*. Paul Chapman: London.

National Numeracy Strategy in Cumbria, The (accessed 2003) www.cleo.net.uk.

Phillips, S., Goodwin, J. and Heron, R. (1998) *Management Skills for SEN Coordinators*. Taylor and Francis: London.

Pollard, A. and Tann, S. (1993) (2nd edn) *Reflective Teaching in the Primary School: A Handbook for the Classroom*. Cassell: London.

Qualifications and Curriculum Authority (1998) *Building Bridges: Guidance and Training Materials for Teachers of Year 6 and Year 7 Pupils*. QCA: London.

School Curriculum and Assessment Authority (1997) *Looking at Children's Learning*. SCAA: London.

Singleton, L. (2000) *Monitoring and Evaluation of the Science Curriculum*. LEA: Leeds.

Smith, R. (2002) *The Primary Headteacher's Handbook*. Kogan Page: London.

TTA (1998) *National Standards for Subject Leaders*. Teacher Training Agency: London.

Tyrrell, J. and Gill, N. (2000) *Coordinating English at Key Stage I*. Falmer Press: London.

Waters, M. (1999) (ed) *Coordinating the Curriculum in the Smaller Primary School*. Falmer Press: London.

Wood D. (1998) (2nd edn) *How Children Think and Learn*. Blackwell: Oxford.